THE SURE TO RISE COOKERY BOOK

LECTOR HOUSE PUBLIC DOMAIN WORKS

THE SURE TO RISE COOKERY BOOK

T. J. EDMONDS

ISBN: 978-93-89509-77-9

Published: 1914

© LECTOR HOUSE LLP

LECTOR HOUSE LLP
E-MAIL: lectorpublishing@gmail.com

THE "SURE TO RISE" COOKERY BOOK

IS ESPECIALLY COMPILED, AND CONTAINS USEFUL EVERYDAY RECIPES, ALSO, COOKING HINTS.

THIRD EDITION of
150,000

POST FREE
TO ANY ADDRESS

COMPILED BY

T. J. EDMONDS,

BAKING POWDER MANUFACTURER,
CHRISTCHURCH.

1914.

THERE'S A RUSH FOR MILK PUDDINGS

When the weather is hot and sultry.

The dish that will then tempt the appetite is the cool, delightful Custard with Milk Pudding or luscious fruit.

Nothing is more delicious than a few stewed peaches, pears or apricots, served with custard made with Edmonds' Custard Powder.

There is no element of uncertainty about the success of the custard—if you use Edmonds' you can take the rest for granted.

Let the children have all the custards they want, and like Oliver Twist, they will be "waiting for more."

CONTENTS

RECIPES

SCONES

PRESERVED GINGER SCONES.

½ lb. flour (one breakfastcup)
1 oz. butter
¼ teaspoon salt
¼ teaspoon sugar
1 teaspoon Edmonds' Baking Powder
Preserved Ginger
Milk and water to mix

Sift baking powder and salt with flour, rub in butter, mix to a stiff dough, turn out on board, cut in two equal parts, roll out, spread one-half with thinly-cut ginger, place the other half on top, cut in squares, brush over the milk, and bake in quick oven.

CINNAMON SCONES.

1 lb. flour
3 teaspoonfuls Edmonds' Baking Powder (moderate)
2 ozs. butter
1 egg
2 teaspoonfuls ground cinnamon
Milk to mix, sugar to taste, salt to taste

Make a light scone mixture, roll out quickly, sprinkle over the cinnamon, fold in three, roll lightly to required thickness, cut into shape, and bake in quick oven.

GIRDLE SCONES.

3 level breakfastcups flour
3 teaspoonfuls Edmonds' Baking Powder
Salt to taste

Mix with large cup of milk and water, divide dough into half, roll out, and cut 4 scones from each. Cook on hot girdle.

YORKSHIRE TEA SCONES.

¾ lb. flour (or 1½ large cups)
1 oz. butter (or a tablespoonful)
1 dessertspoonful sugar
½ cup milk
2 teaspoonfuls Edmonds' Baking Powder
1 egg

Put butter into a saucepan, when dissolved put in the milk, and make warm; place sugar in a basin, and pour on the warm milk. Then place flour in mixing bowl, and mix in Edmonds' Baking Powder, make a well in centre, and drop in the egg, then pour on milk and mix well. The paste should be thin, roll and cut into shapes, place on hot floured oven shelf, and bake in hot oven 10 minutes.

SCOTCH SCONES.

2 breakfastcups flour
2 heaped teaspoons Edmonds' Baking Powder
2 ozs. butter
1 cup milk
Salt to taste

Mix flour and baking powder, then rub in 2 ozs. butter, half a pint milk, mix quickly, roll and cut into shapes, bake in hot oven.

CARRAWAY BISCUITS.

1½ lbs. of flour
½ lb. butter
¾ lb. Sugar
2 eggs
2 teaspoonfuls Edmonds' Baking Powder
2 ozs. currants
2 ozs. candied peel
1 teaspoonful carraway seeds
Little milk

Rub the butter into the flour, add the sugar, baking powder, cleaned currants, carraway seeds, and finely-chopped candied peel. Mix to a stiff paste with the well-beaten eggs, and a little milk. Roll out on a floured board, cut into shapes, and bake in quick oven.

"UP-TO-DATE" BROWN SCONES.

2 breakfastcups of wheatmeal
1 breakfastcup plain flour
3 teaspoonfuls Edmonds' Baking Powder
3 ozs. butter (or lard)
2 heaped dessertspoonfuls sugar
1 egg
Large cup milk. Salt to taste

Mix the wheatmeal, flour, sugar and Edmonds' Baking Powder, then rub in butter (or lard), beat the egg and milk together, and make into stiff dough. Roll and cut into shapes, place on hot floured oven shelf, and bake in quick oven.

SULTANA SCONES.

2 breakfastcups flour
3 moderate teaspoonfuls Edmonds' Baking Powder
2 tablespoonfuls butter
2 dessertspoonfuls sugar
1 egg, half pint milk, salt to taste
1 oz. sultanas or currants

Rub the butter (or lard) into the flour, and add the sugar, sultanas, and baking powder. Beat the egg, and add the milk to it, then mix all together to a wet dough. Roll out on floured board; cut into shapes, and bake in moderate oven 20 minutes.

PLAIN SCONES.

1 breakfastcup flour (piled up)
1½ teaspoons Edmonds' Baking Powder
1 oz. butter (or lard)
1 teaspoon sugar
1 egg

Rub butter (or lard) into flour, then add other dry ingredients, beat egg with little water, mix all into dough. Bake as usual, quick oven. If made without the egg, use milk in place of water.

BREAD AND ROLLS.

COFFEE ROLLS.

3 breakfastcups flour
2 tablespoonfuls butter
3 teaspoonfuls Edmonds' Baking Powder
1 egg
½ pint milk, or more if needed.
1 tablespoonful sugar

Mix baking powder and flour together. Beat butter and sugar to a cream; add egg (beaten), then milk, shape dough oblong, and cut. Make dough same consistency as for scones.

MILK ROLLS.

2 breakfastcups flour
2 tablespoonfuls butter
1 breakfastcup milk
2 heaped teaspoons Edmonds' Baking Powder

Mix into a stiff dough, roll into oblong shape, cut into pieces, brush over with milk, and bake about 20 minutes.

DATE ROLLS.

1 lb. flour (or 2 breakfastcups)
4 ozs. sugar
2 eggs
4 ozs. butter
2 teaspoonfuls Edmonds' Baking Powder
½ lb. dates or sultanas chopped
Milk to mix, salt a pinch, cinnamon

Rub butter into flour, add all dry ingredients, beat egg till frothy, mix all together to a stiff paste, turn out on a board, form into a roll, and cut in equal parts, put on cold, greased, and floured oven tray, and put in quick oven; when nearly done brush over with hot water, and sprinkle liberally with cinnamon and sugar; return to oven to dry.

COTTAGE LOAF.

2 lbs. flour
2 moderate dessertspoonfuls of Edmonds' Prize Baking Powder
½ teaspoonful salt
1 pint milk

Mix the baking powder and salt thoroughly with the flour, and work into light dough with milk. Bake in quick oven.

AERATED BREAD.

To every cup of flour add a heaped teaspoonful of Edmonds' Prize Baking Powder, with a pinch of salt, thoroughly mix while in a dry state, then pour on gradually about half pint of cold water or milk; mix quickly but thoroughly into dough of the usual consistence. Do not knead it more than necessary to mix it perfectly. Make into small loaves, and place immediately in quick oven. (When fully risen open door to let out the steam just a second).

BROWN BREAD.

2 breakfastcups of wheatmeal
1 small cup flour
1 teaspoon sugar
2 heaped teaspoons Edmonds' Baking Powder
1 small teaspoon salt
1 tablespoonful butter
1 breakfastcup milk and water

Mix all the ingredients with the milk and water into dough, turn out and flatten with hand, inch thick, cut four lines across the top, and prick with fork. Bake about 20 minutes.

PUDDINGS.

RICE PUDDING (WITHOUT EGGS).

Stir sufficient rice in boiling water, let boil quarter of an hour, then drain water off, stirring into the boiled rice a cupful of milk and dessertspoonful of sugar. Make a custard (see direction for Custard, page 41), put the rice into a dish, mix thoroughly with the custard while hot. Grate nutmeg on top; bake as usual.

SAGO PUDDING (WITHOUT EGGS).

Stir sufficient sago in boiling water, let boil 15 minutes, then drain water off, stir into the sago a cupful of milk and dessertspoonful sugar; make custard (see direction for Custard, page 41); pour the stewed sago into a dish, mix well with the custard while hot. Grate nutmeg on top; bake as usual.

YORKSHIRE PUDDING.

1 heaped breakfastcup flour
1 pint milk, good measure
½ teaspoon salt
3 eggs
1 tablespoon dripping

Sift flour into a basin, sprinkle salt over it, and make a hole in the middle. Break each egg separately, and stir gradually in, add sufficient milk with wooden spoon until thick batter, then add and mix remainder of milk, and allow the batter to stand for half-an-hour. Place the dripping into a baking dish, make quite hot, and pour in batter; bake slowly for half-hour. A layer of raisins put in bottom of tin before pouring in batter makes a nice raisin Batter Pudding; try this.

BREAD AND BUTTER PUDDING (WITHOUT EGGS).

Slice sufficient white or brown bread (stale) to fill a good-sized pie dish, and spread each slice thinly with butter. Grease the dish, then lay in the slices, sprinkling some currants, sultanas, and sliced candied peel between each layer, adding a little sugar and spice also. Then moisten the bread with a cup of milk. Prepare a pint custard (see direction for Custard, page 41), and pour over while hot, grate nutmeg on; bake as usual.

RASPBERRY PUDDING.

¼ lb. butter
¼ cupful sugar
2 eggs
1 teaspoonful Edmonds' Baking Powder
2 tablespoonfuls raspberry jam
1 breakfastcup flour

MODE.—Beat butter and sugar to a cream, add eggs (well beaten), then the flour, baking powder and jam; put into a buttered basin, and steam 2½ hours.

DATE PUDDING.

3 ozs. butter
6 ozs. flour
2 or 3 eggs
1 small teaspoon Edmonds' Baking Powder
4 ozs. sugar
4 ozs. dates
3 tablespoons milk
1 teaspoon lemon juice

MODE.—Beat butter and sugar to a cream, add eggs, and beat well. Then add milk, dates (chopped up fine), lemon juice, and last sift in the flour and baking powder mixed. Steam 2 hours in a buttered mould.

RITA'S APPLE PUDDING.

Mix thoroughly a teaspoon of Edmonds' Baking Powder with a breakfastcup of flour. Beat 2 eggs well, add 1 gill of milk, and a tablespoon of butter, beat all together 15 minutes. Place 2 inches of stewed apples (sweetened) in a pie dish. Pour in batter, and bake in quick oven; serve hot.

FRUIT PUDDING.

1 small cup sugar
2 breakfastcups flour
1 tablespoonful butter
2 eggs
2 teaspoonfuls Edmonds' Baking Powder
¾ cup milk (or more)

Beat butter and sugar to a cream, add eggs (beaten) and milk. Mix flour and baking powder together, and add to mixture. Grease two small dishes, fill half full of fresh fruit, pour over the batter; bake 1 hour.

AMERICAN PUDDING.

4 apples
½ pint milk
2 eggs

1 tablespoon flour
½ nutmeg
1 tablespoon minced suet
½ teaspoon Edmonds' Baking Powder
Sugar, sweeten to taste

Core and halve the apples, beat eggs, add flour, baking powder and milk. Grease a pie dish; lay the apples in (cut part down), pour the mixture over, then sprinkle in the minced suet, and grate nutmeg on top. Bake moderate half-hour.

DOMINION PUDDING.

1 breakfastcup flour
½ breakfastcup sugar
1 tablespoonful butter
1 egg
½ cupful sweet milk
1 teaspoon Edmonds' Baking Powder

Rub butter into flour and Edmonds' Baking Powder, add sugar, beat egg and milk together, and mix all into batter. Place some raisins at bottom of mould or basin, pour batter over, and steam for 1¼ hours.

BEEF STEAK PUDDING.

½ lb. bread crumbs
½ lb. flour
1 teaspoonful Edmonds' Baking Powder
1 lb. of steak
½ lb. suet
3 kidneys
Seasoning

Mix crumbs, flour, suet, salt to taste, and baking powder, with enough cold water to make stiff paste. Roll out and line a basin, leaving a small hole at the bottom of paste. Cut steak up and dredge with flour. Cut kidney small; add pepper and seasoning; cover with a thick layer of paste, and boil about 3 hours.

COCOANUT CUSTARD.

Put small teacupful of desiccated cocoanut in pie-dish, then make a pint custard of 2 eggs, and pint of milk, with two dessertspoonfuls sugar. Pour over cocoanut, and bake as usual.

SUET DUMPLINGS.

1 teacupful flour
2 tablespoonfuls chopped suet
Cold water
pepper and salt to taste

½ teaspoon Edmonds' Baking Powder
1 dessertspoonful chopped parsley

Mix all the dry ingredients, rubbing suet into the flour, and make all into stiff paste with cold water. Cut and roll into balls, covering the outsides with flour, which prevents breaking. When ready, drop them into the stew, which must be boiling slowly, and cook for half-hour longer.

APPLE DUMPLINGS.

3 ozs. flour
½ teaspoon Edmonds' Baking Powder
3 apples
3 ozs. suet
3 ozs. breadcrumbs
¼ teaspoon salt
3 dessertspoonfuls sugar

Prepare the apples, make a paste of flour, suet, breadcrumbs, add baking powder, salt, and water to mix. Place a piece of paste round each apple, put dessertspoonful sugar in each, then cover the top. Put dumplings loose into pan of boiling water, when they come to surface give them ½ hour.

ROLLED FRENCH PUDDING.

Roll out a nice suet crust as for rolly poly, scatter over some chopped figs, dates, apple or lemon juice, finely chopped candied peel, breadcrumbs, golden syrup, ground ginger, and nutmeg, little pieces of butter here and there, roll up, secure ends, tie in cloth, and boil about 2 hours; put pudding into boiling water.

BAKED JAM ROLL.

½ lb. flour
4 ozs. dripping (or lard or butter)
Salt a little
½ teaspoon Edmonds' Baking Powder
½ teaspoon Sugar (fine)
Water to mix

Beat butter (or dripping) to a cream, add all other ingredients, and sufficient water to make a dough, roll out into shape, and spread with apricot or raspberry jam, sliced apples, plums, or any fruit desired could be substituted for jam. Put in a baking dish; bake in moderate oven.

HENDY PUDDING.

1 cup suet (chopped)
2 breakfastcups flour
¼ breakfastcup sugar
2 teaspoons Edmonds' Baking Powder (heaped)

Jam, water to mix

Mix all dry ingredients with water to a stiff dough, which divide into three, place alternately in greased basin a layer of dough, then jam, steam 3 hours. Serve with sweet or jam sauce.

BAKED APPLE DUMPLINGS.

1 lb. flour (or 2 breakfastcups)
½ lb. butter (or dripping)
½ teaspoon Edmonds' Baking Powder
Water to mix

Pare and core the apples, fill cavity with sugar and nutmeg, roll each separately in paste, put in baking dish, and quarter cover with hot water containing half cup sugar, one ounce of butter, one tablespoonful of Golden Syrup. Baste frequently, allow three-quarters of an hour to bake, try with skewer; serve with custard or cream.

CHRISTMAS PLUM PUDDING.

¾ lb. flour (or 1½ breakfastcups)
2 heaped teaspoonfuls Edmonds' Baking Powder
2 ozs. stale bread crumbs
1½ lb. suet
2 lbs. raisins
1 lb. currants
6 eggs
10 ozs. sugar (brown)
¼ lb. almonds
½ lb. mixed candied peel
Salt and spice to taste

Mix ingredients well together, and add 6 eggs well beaten, and three-quarters of a pint of milk; divide into two, and boil 8 hours, or four, and boil 6 hours.

DOUGHNUTS.

3½ breakfastcups flour
1 breakfastcup sugar
½ breakfastcup butter
4 eggs
1 cup milk
3 teaspoonfuls Edmonds' Baking Powder
½ teaspoonful salt

Beat sugar and eggs together in a separate basin, rub butter into flour, add salt and baking powder, mix well, then mix flour with the eggs and sugar, roll out, cut into rounds, and fry in hot lard; serve hot.

"LOVE IN A ——"

"Do you love me?" said the cup to the custard.
"I'm just brimming up in you," replied the custard.
"You sweet thing," answered the cup.
"Delightful."

A GOLDEN RULE.—Hold fast to that which is good.

PASTRY.

MINCE PIES.

INGREDIENTS.—Mince meat, a sufficiency, and puff or short paste Recipes (see page 18).

Roll out the paste to a suitable thickness, line with it the patty pans, previously well buttered; put in each sufficient mince meat, make lids of paste, cover over, press lightly at the edges, neatly trim round with a knife, and bake in a moderately quick oven. When done, sprinkle with powdered white sugar.

MINCE MEAT.

2 lbs. apples (pared and cored)
2 lbs. raisins (stoned)
2 lbs. currants
2 lbs. suet (chopped fine)
¾ lb. mixed candied peel (chopped)
½ lb. sugar
½ pint brandy (or 1 breakfastcup)
¼ pint sherry (or ½ breakfastcup)
1 small nutmeg (grated)
1 dessertspoonful powdered cinnamon
1 dessertspoonful salt
The juice of two small oranges
The juice of two small lemons
The peel of one each grated

Put apples and raisins through mincer, then mix with all other ingredients well together, put into jars, with piece of paper on top dipped in brandy, then cover.

MARMALADE CHEESE CAKES.

2 tablespoonfuls marmalade
2 eggs
2 ozs. butter

Melt the butter, beat the eggs, and add to marmalade. Line patty pans with puff paste (see recipe page 18), pour in the mixture, and bake in a quick oven.

PLAIN PUFF PASTRY.

½ lb. flour
7 ozs. butter
½ teaspoonful Edmonds' Baking Powder
Water to mix

Mode.—Place the flour on a pastry-board with the butter, chop the butter into the flour with a knife, then put into a basin, add baking powder, and sufficient water to make a soft dough. Roll out several times.

SHORT PASTRY.

1 breakfastcup flour, pinch salt
4 ozs. butter or lard
½ teaspoonful Edmonds' Baking Powder
Water to mix

Mode.—Rub the butter into the flour, add salt, baking powder, and water a little at a time to make a firm dough. Roll out to required thickness.

YORKSHIRE CHEESE CAKES.

1 teacup curds
1 oz. butter
1 oz. sugar
1 egg
1 tablespoon currants

Mode.—Cream butter and sugar, mix with the curds, mix all ingredients together. Fill patty-pans, lined with pastry.

To prepare the curd, boil 2 quarts of milk, and as it rises pour in either ½ pint of vinegar or buttermilk to turn it to curds. Draw the pan to side of the fire, let it stand 5 minutes, then strain through a sieve.

Pastry requires a hot oven; if it contains baking powder—must be baked at once.

APPLE SANDWICH.

½ lb. butter
1 lb. flour
2 teaspoonfuls Edmonds' Baking Powder
Mince 2 or 3 apples
1 cupful clean currants
1 piece of peel
1 dessertspoonful cinnamon
1 lemon
1 egg
2 tablespoons sugar

Mode.—Rub butter into flour, then add baking powder, make into a firm dough with water. Roll out to required thickness; mince all other ingredients together, and mix in egg last. Place mince between pastry, and bake.

A GOOD PIE CRUST.

4 breakfastcups flour
2 heaped teaspoonfuls Edmonds' Baking Powder
1 level teaspoon salt
1 lb. butter (lard or dripping may be used)

Mix well together, then add 2 cups of water, and roll out. This makes light paste for pies, tarts, custard, etc.

CORNISH PASTY.

¼ lb. pastry
1 teacupful raw potato
1 teacupful raw meat
A small piece of onion chopped fine
½ teaspoonful salt
¼ teaspoonful pepper
3 tablespoonfuls cold water or gravy

Mix all ingredients together on a plate, roll pastry into an oval shape, put the mixture on the paste, wet the edges on the top, and prick well. Brush over a little egg or milk, and bake in a hot oven for about half-an-hour.

TESTIMONIALS.

— — — — — —

Taumarunui,
Nov. 8th, 1911.

T. J. Edmonds, Esq.,
Christchurch.

Dear Sir,—At the Levin and Horowhenua Autumn Shows I was awarded 10 Firsts, 3 Seconds, and 2 Highly Commended Prizes for Cakes, etc., made with your Baking Powder. I always recommend your Powder, as it is the best I have used.

Yours faithfully,
MRS. H. BROMLEY.

— — — — — —

17 Oxford Street,
South Dunedin.

To T. J. Edmonds,

I have used your Baking Powder for 14 years, and would not

think of using any other. When I first asked my grocer for it, he did not know anything about it, so he sent to Christchurch for it, and now has good sales. I have introduced it to many of my friends, and all are more than satisfied. My daughter-in-law received Second Prize in the Winter Show the first year she competed; she used your Powder.

Yours etc.,
MRS. SEYMOUR.

———————

Kia Ora Tea Rooms,
Tahunanui,
Nelson.

Mr. T. J. Edmonds.

Dear Sir,—After using "Edmonds' Prize Baking Powder" for a period extending over ten years, I have come to the conclusion that it is the best on the market, and highly recommend all who have not tried it to do so without delay.

MRS. T. J. WILSON.

March 23rd, 1911.

———————

Kaponga,
Taranaki.

Mr. Edmonds.

Dear Sir,—I have been a big user of your Baking Powder for the last seven years. I have won prizes at various Shows for my cooking, and I have always used your Baking Powder. I use 1½ tins a month, and always refuse any other offered to me.

MRS. A. T. PHILLIPS.

CAKES AND BUNS.

ENGLISH QUEEN CAKES.

4 eggs
Their weight in butter, sugar and flour
1 teaspoon Edmonds' Baking Powder
4 ozs. currants
Flavouring to taste

Beat butter and sugar to a cream, then beat in eggs. Mix currants with flour and baking powder, and add to mixture. Bake in hot oven.

RASPBERRY DELIGHTS.

2 tablespoonfuls sugar
1 egg
2 tablespoonfuls butter
½ teaspoonful Edmonds' Baking Powder
1 teaspoonful flour
1 tablespoonful Edmonds' Custard Powder

Mode.—Cream butter and sugar together, add the egg; mix flour, baking, and custard powder together, and add by degrees to mixture. Place in greased patty-tins on cold oven shelf, and bake ten minutes. When nearly baked, place a teaspoonful of raspberry jam on each, and then bake a little longer.

CHELSEA BUNS.

2 breakfastcups flour
2 heaped teaspoons Edmonds' Prize Baking Powder
2 tablespoonfuls sugar
2 tablespoonfuls butter
1 egg
Spice, and milk to mix

Rub all dry ingredients together, mix with milk to desired paste, roll out, cover with spice, and sugar, and bake as usual.

ALMOND FINGERS.

1 breakfastcup of flour
¼ lb. butter

2 ozs. sugar
1 egg
1 teaspoon Edmonds' Baking Powder

Beat butter and sugar to a cream, add yolk of egg, and beat well. Mix flour and baking powder together, and add to mixture with the hand. Paste must be very stiff. Roll out thin. Make the icing with the white of the egg, spread on top of paste. Place chopped almonds on. Cut into fingers; bake moderate oven.

RICH PLUM CAKE.

Take ½ lb. butter, and ½ lb. sugar, beat these well together with the hand to a cream, add 4 eggs, one at a time, beat well into the butter and sugar, lightly mix in 2 breakfastcups of flour previously mixed with one heaped teaspoon of Edmonds' Baking Powder, then lightly mix in ½ lb. sultanas. Bake at once thoroughly in fairly quick oven.

BUFFALO CAKE.

1¼ breakfastcups flour
¼ lb. butter
2 eggs
¾ breakfastcup sugar
2 teaspoonfuls Edmonds' Baking Powder

Cream butter and sugar, add eggs beaten, mix flour and baking powder, and add to mixture, then enough milk to make thin. Cook in sponge sandwich tins. Put together with lemon honey or raspberry jam. Icing on top.

SMALL CAKES (WITHOUT EGGS).

3 ozs. butter (or dripping)
3 ozs. sugar
½ lb. flour (or 1 breakfastcup)
1 teaspoonful ground ginger
1 heaped teaspoonful Edmonds' Egg Powder
Milk to mix about ¼ pint.

Soften butter or dripping if very hard, add sugar and beat to a cream. Slightly warm the milk, and beat it in by degrees. Stir in lightly the flour previously sifted with the Egg powder, ground ginger, and half a saltspoon of salt, drop in spoonfuls on a cold baking tray, sprinkle a little sugar over, and bake in hot oven for about ten minutes. The mixture for these and all eggless cakes must be fairly firm, and the spoonfuls piled high on the baking tray.

ELSIE'S FINGERS.

¼ lb. butter
3 ozs. sugar
2 small cups flour

1½ teaspoonfuls Baking Powder (Edmonds')
1 egg

Beat butter and sugar, add egg and flour mixed with baking powder, roll small pieces between the hands, dip in sugar, and put on cold tray; bake in moderate oven till slightly brown.

PIKELETS.

1 breakfastcup flour
1 dessertspoonful sugar
1 egg (well beaten)
1 teaspoon Edmonds' Baking Powder
¾ breakfastcup milk
1 oz. butter

Mix flour, sugar, and Edmonds' Baking Powder together, then mix egg and milk, make a well in centre of dry ingredients, and mix to a smooth paste with milk. Cook in small lots on hot greased girdle.

RENE'S KISSES.

½ lb. cornflour
½ lb. butter
½ lb. sugar
½ lb. flour
4 eggs

2 teaspoonfuls Edmonds' Baking Powder

Cream butter and sugar, add eggs beaten and flavouring, mix baking powder, flour, and cornflour, and add to mixture; mix until quite light, drop in teaspoon lots on cold oven shelf, bake in quick oven; when cold, fasten together with jam.

SPONGE SANDWICH.

3 eggs
1 cup sugar (small)
1 cup flour (small)
½ teaspoon Edmonds' Baking Powder

Beat eggs and sugar well, then add flour and baking powder mixed; bake in hot oven in sandwich tins.

SPONGE ROLL.

1 cup flour
1 tea cup sugar
3 eggs
1 teaspoon Edmonds' Baking Powder
2 tablespoons cold water

Method.—Beat eggs and sugar till stiff and frothy, sift flour and baking powder, add water to eggs and sugar, then stir in the sifted flour and baking powder lightly and quickly, pour into greased tin, and bake in hot oven from 8 to 10 minutes. This recipe will also serve for a Jam Sandwich.

CHRISTMAS CAKE.

1 lb. butter
1 lb. currants
1 lb. raisins
1 lb. sultanas
¼ lb. mixed peel
¼ lb. almonds
4 breakfastcups flour
2 breakfastcups sugar
10 eggs
1 heaped teaspoon Edmonds' Baking Powder
Wine glass brandy

Beat butter to a cream, add sugar, then eggs one by one (unbeaten); mix baking powder with flour, and put in, then fruit dredged with flour. Brandy. Cook 4½ hours, moderate oven.

EXPRESS CAKES.

1 breakfastcup flour
1 teacup sugar

2 teaspoonfuls Edmonds' Baking Powder
3 eggs
¼ cup milk
(Essence vanilla or lemon)

Mix flour, sugar, and Edmonds' baking powder together, beat in the eggs and milk, put into small greased tins. Bake in moderate oven about 20 minutes.

NEW ZEALAND BUNS.

1 breakfastcup flour
1 tablespoonful sugar
1 heaped teaspoon Edmonds' Baking Powder
1 egg
3 ozs. butter

Rub the butter into flour, sugar, and baking powder, then add the egg well beaten, and enough milk to make a stiff dough. Place in heaps on cold greased oven shelf. Bake quick oven 10 to 15 minutes.

SPONGE CAKE.

2 level breakfastcups flour
1 level breakfastcup sugar
4 tablespoons milk
2 teaspoons Edmonds' Prize Baking Powder
4 eggs
Pinch salt

Beat the eggs, then beat in the sugar, add salt and milk. Mix flour and powder together in dry state, then sift it in; beat all together, and bake in quick oven.

ROCK CAKES.

1 breakfastcup flour
2 heaped dessertspoonfuls sugar
2 ozs. currants
2 ozs. butter (or lard)
1 oz. or 1 round candied peel
1 dessertspoonful Edmonds' Baking Powder
Milk to mix

Rub the butter (or lard) into flour, then add other dry ingredients, the egg beaten, and sufficient milk to make stiff dough. Place in rocky shapes on cold greased oven shelf, and bake in hot oven 10 or 12 minutes.

CHILDREN'S CAKES.

2 breakfastcups flour
3 ozs. dripping
1 teaspoonful Edmonds' Baking Powder

¼ lb. sugar
¼ lb. sultanas
1 oz. peel
½ teaspoonful salt
1 egg

MODE.—Rub dripping well into the flour, add all dry ingredients. Beat the egg well, mix with a breakfastcup nearly full of milk. Mix all together, and bake in greased patty-tins about 15 minutes.

SHORTBREAD.

½ lb. flour (or one breakfastcup)
¼ lb. butter
2 ozs. sugar (or 2 tablespoonfuls)

Cream butter and sugar, then work in the flour, continue to work until it becomes a firm dough. Place into an ungreased tin, press well down with the knuckles, then smooth over with a knife, and prick with fork. Bake in a slow oven 1 hour. Cut into shapes whilst hot in the tin.

FRUIT CAKE.

2 breakfastcups flour
½ lb. butter
½ lb. sugar
1 teaspoon Edmonds' Baking Powder
8 eggs
1 teaspoon ground nutmeg
1 lb. currants
4 ozs. almonds
½ lb. mixed peel

MODE.—Beat butter to a cream, add sugar gradually, then white of eggs (beaten 10 minutes), then yolks (beaten 10 minutes), then flour and other ingredients. Bake 2½ hours moderate oven.

RICE CAKES.

1 cup flour
½ cup ground rice
¼ lb. sugar
3 ozs. butter
1 egg
½ cup milk
1 teaspoonful Edmonds' Baking Powder
A pinch of salt

Cream butter and sugar, sift dry ingredients together, whisk the egg well, and mix all thoroughly. Add flavouring, and a few currants if liked. Bake in patty pans in moderate oven about 10 minutes.

SUNBEAM CAKE.

½ lb. sugar
½ lb. butter
½ lb. sultanas
¼ lb. peel
¾ lb. flour
6 eggs
1 small teaspoonful Edmonds' Baking Powder
A few almonds and flavouring

MODE.—Whip butter and sugar to a cream, beat in eggs one by one, then add flour and baking powder, fruit, peel, almonds, and flavouring. Bake in moderate oven 2 hours.

PANCAKES.

2 breakfastcups flour
2 teaspoonfuls Edmonds' Prize Baking Powder
Pinch of salt

Mix well in dry state, add two eggs, well beaten, and enough milk to make thin batter. Fry with lard or butter.

GRATED NUT CAKES.

1½ breakfastcups flour
¼ lb. desiccated cocoanut (or almonds)
6 tablespoonfuls sugar
4 ozs. butter
½ teacup milk
1 dessertspoonful Edmonds' Egg Powder

Mix cocoanut with the flour, sugar, and Egg Powder. Soften the butter a little, then rub it lightly into the other ingredients, moisten the whole with the milk slightly warmed, and bake in moderate quick oven in buttered patty pans.

AFTERNOON TEA CAKES.

1 breakfastcup flour
2 heaped dessertspoonfuls sugar
3 ozs. butter (or 3 tablespoonfuls)
1 egg (well beaten) and some milk
1 teaspoon Edmonds' Baking Powder
Jam (raspberry preferred)

Rub butter into flour, then add sugar and Edmonds' Baking Powder, mix well, add egg and sufficient milk to make a light dough. Roll and cut into rounds; place a little raspberry jam on each, wet the edges, and press them together. Put on cold, greased oven shelf, and bake about 10 minutes.

RICE CAKES (WITHOUT EGGS).

1 cup flour
½ cup ground rice
¼ lb. sugar
4 ozs. butter
½ cup milk (good measure)
1 heaped teaspoonful Edmonds' Egg Powder
Pinch salt

Cream butter and sugar, sift and mix dry ingredients into same, mix all thoroughly with the milk, add flavouring, and bake in patty pans in moderate oven from 10 to 12 minutes.

WALNUT CAKE.

1 large cup flour
1 small cup sugar
1 small cup butter
1 tablespoon cocoa
1 teaspoon Edmonds' Baking Powder
1 cup walnuts
3 eggs

Beat butter and sugar to a cream, add eggs well beaten, mix cocoa with a little milk, then add the other ingredients, and bake in shallow cake tin in moderate oven. When cold, ice with water icing, and place some walnuts halved on top.

Currants should be rubbed in a colander with a little flour before using.

A GOOD PLAIN CAKE.

Mix well together two breakfastcups of flour, two teaspoonfuls Edmonds' Baking Powder, a little salt and spice, and ¼ lb. sugar. Rub in ½ lb. butter, then mix in 6 ozs. sultanas, 2 ozs. currants, a few pieces sliced peel. Beat 3 eggs and half-cupful milk together, and moisten the lot. Bake in quick oven thoroughly.

CHOCOLATE CAKES.

¼ lb. flour
¼ lb. sugar
2 eggs
2 tablespoonfuls butter
1 teaspoon chocolate (or 1½ teaspoons cocoa)
½ teaspoonful vanilla essence
½ teaspoonful Edmonds' Prize Baking Powder

Beat butter and sugar together, then add flour, baking powder, cocoa and essence. Bake in moderate oven 15 to 20 minutes in sandwich tins. Ice with chocolate icing.

LEMON BISCUITS.

½ lb. butter
½ lb. sugar
1 lb. (or 2 breakfastcups) flour
2 eggs
1 teaspoonful Edmonds' Baking Powder
Flavour with essence of lemon

Cream butter and sugar together, add eggs, then flour and powder mixed well, roll out thin, cut into shapes and bake.

MADEIRA CAKE.

3 eggs, their weight in butter and sugar
The weight of 4 eggs in flour
1 teaspoonful Edmonds' Baking Powder
Juice of one small lemon

Cream butter and sugar, add eggs one by one, beat well, add lemon juice, flour, and baking powder. Bake in buttered cake tin in moderate oven for about one hour. Ice the top if desired.

DATE CAKE.

½ lb. butter
½ lb. sugar
6 eggs
½ lb. dates
1½ breakfastcups flour
1 teaspoonful Edmonds' Baking Powder

Beat butter and sugar to a cream, add eggs 2 at a time; beat well, add flour, powder, and fruit. Bake about 1½ hours.

PYRAMIDS.

1 breakfastcup flour
2 teaspoonfuls Edmonds' Baking Powder
1 teaspoonful cornflour (or potato flour)
¼ lb. sugar
¼ lb. butter
4 eggs
Flavouring

Beat butter and sugar to a cream, well whisk the eggs, sift dry ingredients together, make a hole in centre of flour, in which put butter and eggs, mix thoroughly but lightly; add flavouring liked, and bake in small patty pans in hot oven for about 10 minutes.

PICNIC DAINTIES.

1½ breakfastcups flour
3 tablespoonfuls butter
2 tablespoonfuls sugar
1 dessertspoonful Edmonds' Egg Powder
Milk to mix

Rub butter into flour, then stir in sugar, egg powder and sufficient milk to make firm dough. Roll and cut into rounds, place one teaspoonful of raspberry jam in the centre; wet the edges and press them together. Place on cold greased oven shelf. Bake 12 minutes.

SEED CAKE.

½ lb. butter
½ lb. sugar
6 eggs
2 cups flour
1 teaspoonful Edmonds' Baking Powder
Caraway seed, lemon peel

Beat butter and sugar to a cream, then add the eggs, beating in one by one with the hand; lastly, add flour and baking powder, mixed together, with seeds and lemon peel as desired.

GINGER CAKE.

2 breakfastcups flour
1 teacup sugar
1 teaspoon baking soda
1 teaspoon Edmonds' Baking Powder
1 teacup golden syrup
1 teacup butter
1 teacup milk
2 eggs
2 dessertspoonfuls ground ginger
1 teaspoonful cinnamon
½ teaspoonful spice

Mix dry ingredients, add eggs well beaten, and butter (melted) last of all; bake three-quarters of an hour.

VICTORIA SANDWICH.

2 level breakfastcups flour
1 level breakfastcup sugar
4 ozs. butter
3 eggs
2 teaspoons Edmonds' Baking Powder

1 small cup water
Essence flavouring to taste

Warm the butter, and beat in the sugar, drop in the eggs one at a time, then the flour with the baking powder mixed, must be lightly beaten in; add flavouring and water gradually. The baking powder may be added last of all to give better results. Bake in quick oven 15 minutes.

SULTANA CAKE.

1 lb. flour
½ lb. butter
½ lb. sultanas
½ lb. sugar
4 eggs
3 ozs. peel
1 heaped teaspoonful Edmonds' Baking Powder
A little milk

Cream the butter and sugar together, add eggs well beaten, then the other ingredients; bake in moderate oven two hours

GIRDLE CAKES.

Rub into two breakfastcups flour 6 ozs. of butter, add 3 teaspoonfuls Edmonds' Baking Powder, and mix thoroughly. Mix into this ¼ lb. currants, pinch salt, a little nutmeg, and make into light dough with milk. Roll out, cut into rounds, bake 15 minutes on a girdle or in the oven. If required sweet, add tablespoonful sugar.

LEMON TEA CAKES.

Rub into 1½ breakfastcups of flour 3 tablespoonfuls each of lard and butter; add 6 ozs. moist sugar, the grated rind of one lemon, a little of the juice, and a heaped teaspoonful of Edmonds' Prize Baking Powder. Mix into moderate paste, with 2 well beaten eggs. Divide into cakes; place on greased oven shelf, and bake in brisk oven 20 minutes.

TEA CAKES (WITHOUT EGGS).

1 lb. flour
4 ozs. sugar
4 ozs. butter
2 teaspoonfuls Edmonds' Egg Powder
½ lb. dates (or sultanas) chopped
Milk to mix, salt a pinch

Rub butter into flour, add all dry ingredients, mix all together to a paste with milk, turn out on board, form into a roll, and cut in equal parts, put on cold greased and floured tray, and bake in quick oven.

TENNIS BUNS.

1 breakfastcup flour
3 heaped dessertspoonfuls sugar
1 teaspoon Edmonds' Baking Powder
1 egg
3 ozs. butter
Candied peel and milk
Essence of lemon to taste

Rub butter into flour, add other dry ingredients, mix well, then add the egg well beaten, and enough milk to make a stiff dough. Place in small lots on a cold greased oven shelf. Put a piece of candied peel on top of each. Bake in quick oven about 10 minutes.

"EGG POWDER" ROCK CAKES.

1 breakfastcup flour
2 dessertspoonfuls sugar
2 ozs. currants
4 ozs. butter (or lard)
½ oz. or 1 round candied peel
1 dessertspoonful Edmond's Egg Powder
Milk to mix

Rub the butter (or lard) into flour, add the other dry ingredients, and sufficient milk to make a stiff dough, place on cold greased oven shelf in rocky shapes. Bake in hot oven.

SMALL COCOANUT CAKES.

1 breakfastcup flour
4 ozs. desiccated cocoanut
2 dessertspoonfuls sugar
1 teaspoon Edmonds' Baking Powder
2 ozs butter (or 2 tablespoonfuls)
Milk

Rub butter into flour, mix in cocoanut, Edmonds' baking powder, and sugar, making into stiff dough with milk. Place in small lots on cold greased oven shelf, and bake in hot oven about 20 minutes.

EXCELLENT FOR SUPPERS.

Edmonds' Custards, served hot (grate little nutmeg on top to taste), are delicious also for children's parties.

A tablespoonful of flour equals 1 ounce, and so on. One large breakfastcup of flour equals half pound.

TO YOUNG PEOPLE.

To make sure that cakes are baked enough, stick a clean bright skewer, or straw through it; if it comes out clean and free from the cake mixture it is done, if otherwise, it requires longer cooking. Careful practice will bring you success.

COFFEE CAKE.

¼ lb. butter (or dripping)
¼ lb. sugar
½ cup Golden Syrup
1 large cup of strong coffee
1 lb. flour (or 2 breakfastcups)
2 heaped teaspoonfuls Edmonds' Baking Powder
1 teaspoonful ground ginger
A few raisins and peel
A little spice or nutmeg

Cream butter and sugar, add syrup warmed and mixed with the coffee, together with sifted flour, add spices to creamed butter, add raisins and peel, then beat in baking powder; bake in moderate oven about 2 hours.

BATH BUNS.

½ cupful butter
1 cupful sugar
3 eggs
½ cupful lemon peel (cut up)
3 breakfastcups flour
3 teaspoons Edmonds' Baking Powder

Beat butter and sugar to a cream, add the eggs, and beat few minutes longer, add other ingredients, and mix into moderate paste with milk. Place on cold oven shelf (greased), and bake about 12 or 15 minutes in hot oven.

Special.—If Edmonds' Baking Powder should appear lumpy in tin, it will easily powder up again (with back of spoon) before using in cooking.

ABOUT CAKE MIXING.

Always cream together the butter and sugar in a basin, before commencing to add the eggs already beaten; this will add success to your cakes.

COCOANUT DELICACIES.

½ breakfastcup flour (or ¼ lb.)
½ breakfastcup cocoanut (or ¼ lb.) desiccated
3 ozs. butter (or 3 tablespoonfuls)
2 heaped dessertspoonfuls sugar
1 egg
1 teaspoon Edmonds' Baking Powder

Rub butter into flour, add other dry ingredients, and mix, then add egg beaten, this should make stiff dough (if not add very little milk, as dough must be stiff). Place on cold greased oven shelf in small lots. Bake in hot oven from 10 to 12 minutes.

A RIDDLE

For the young generations and new arrivals in the Dominion.

WHY IS
EDMONDS'
. . . PRIZE. . .
BAKING POWDER
"LIKE THE SUN?"

Send us your name and address when you require a new Cookery Book. Posted Free.

EDMONDS' BAKING POWDER WORKS,
Christchurch.

To soften scones always turn out on clean towel, and cover them with the ends.

MISCELLANEOUS.

DELICIOUS TRIFLE.

Cut up stale sponge cakes in dish, spread over with jam (raspberry preferred), then make a pint custard, (as per direction for Custard), and pour when cooked over the cakes. Let stand till cold, then spread whipped cream on top. This dish is improved by adding a little sherry or wine to the cut sponges.

EGG DRINK (WITHOUT EGGS).

Two large cups of milk; take sufficient to mix smooth 1 heaped teaspoon of Edmonds' Custard Powder. Place remainder in saucepan with 2 teaspoonfuls sugar; when it boils add mixture, stir and place immediately into glasses (grate nutmeg on top to taste).

TO MAKE A CUSTARD.

From a pint of new milk take enough to mix smooth one large dessertspoonful of Edmonds' Custard Powder, sweeten the remainder of the milk to taste (say, a heaped dessertspoonful sugar), and when the milk is boiling, pour the mixed custard into it, stir and pour immediately into jug. When cold, place in glasses (grate nutmeg on if desired).

PEAR GINGER.

6 lb. pears (nearly ripe)
1 lb. preserved ginger (full lb.)
4 lbs. sugar

Cut up pears, and let stand over night with sugar on, boil with ginger following day until soft.

LEMON HONEY (FOR SPONGES OR TARTS).

1 lb. sugar
Rind and juice of 4 lemons
4 ozs. butter
4 eggs

Grate only the yellow part of the lemon rinds (avoid white part, as it is bitter), strain the juice, beat eggs a little, put all ingredients into enamelled pot; cook slowly until thick and smooth. Do not let it boil. Put in jar, and cover when cold.

LEMON SPONGE.

½ packet isinglass or gelatine
5 ozs. loaf sugar
¾ pint cold water
2 lemons
Whites of 2 eggs

Soak the isinglass or gelatine in ¾ pint cold water, then dissolve over the fire with the rind of two lemons thinly pared, add the sugar and the juice of 2 lemons. Boil all together 2 or 3 minutes; strain and let it remain until nearly cold, and beginning to set, then add the white of 2 eggs, well beaten, and whisk 10 minutes, when it will become the consistence of sponge; put it lightly into a glass dish immediately, leaving it in appearance as rocky as possible.

All fruit sponges are made in the same way. If syrups are used for flavouring, use ¾ oz. gelatine.

EDMONDS' CUSTARD, WITH STEWED PRUNES AND FIGS.

Barely cover fruit with water, and sugar to taste. Simmer till tender (with no addition of water), then serve either hot or cold, with custard.

(To make custard, see page 30).

PINEAPPLE JELLY.

1 tin pineapple chunks
2 packets White's jelly crystals

Cut up pineapple into small dice, dividing fruit and juice into two jelly moulds; make jellies separately, using little less water than directed, then pour into moulds.

FIG AND BANANA SALAD.

Slice in equal quantities some nice bananas and freshly preserved figs, sprinkle castor sugar over each layer, add lemon juice if desired, place in glass dish, and cover with whipped cream flavoured with vanilla, put in a cool place for 2 hours.

BAKED PEARS.

Pears
Golden syrup
Water

Wipe some large sound pears, arrange them in an enamel baking dish with stalk ends upwards, pour a little water over them, and enough golden syrup to sweeten (say one tablespoonful to every three pears). Bake in a slow oven 2 hours or more. If baked slowly they will be juicy, tender and sweet, baste them frequently with the syrup and water, if oven is too hot cover with oven shelf. Serve with cream or custard.

TOMATO AND MACARONI.

¼ lb. macaroni
Tomatoes, onion, butter
Pepper and salt

Break up macaroni and boil in plenty of water slightly salted, boil one onion in the same water, strain and put a layer in a buttered pie dish, put next a layer of sliced tomato and the boiled onion, another layer of macaroni, and so on with pepper and salt on each layer till dish is full; have tomato on top layer, sprinkle bread crumbs over, and some little pieces of butter. Bake till tomatoes are cooked about one hour.

TOMATO SOUP.

2 lbs. tomatoes
1 oz. butter
2 ozs. sago
1 large onion
1 quart stock
Pepper and salt

Slice the tomatoes and onion, and boil in stock until tender, strain through a colander, and return to the saucepan, then add butter, sago, and seasoning; boil till sago is cooked.

WHITE SAUCE.

Boil 1 pint of rich milk. Stir into it 1 tablespoonful of flour, previously made smooth in a little milk. To this add salt (and, if preferred, 1 teaspoonful of olive oil). Serve hot. For parsley sauce, just add before serving half teaspoonful of finely-chopped parsley.

TOMATO SAUCE (NO. 1).

12 lbs. tomatoes
2 lbs. onions
2 ozs. garlic (chopped fine)
1 oz. ground ginger
½ oz. cloves
4 ozs. salt
½ oz. cayenne pepper

Place spices in a bag, and boil with rest of ingredients 2 hours (occasionally squeeze the spice bag), then beat through a sieve or colander till nothing but skin and seed remains. When cool, add a quart of best malt vinegar, half a lb. brown sugar, boil again until it is as thick as cream. Bottle and cork when cold. Always put sauce in small bottles if convenient, it keeps better, and seal top of same.

TOMATO SAUCE (NO. 2).

12 lbs. tomatoes
2 lb. cooking apples
1 lb. onions
¾ lb. sugar
¼ lb. salt
2 ozs. each of allspice and garlic
¼ oz. each of chillies, mace and cloves
1 quart best English malt vinegar

Wipe and break the tomatoes, cut up garlic, apples, and onions. Boil all together with rest of ingredients 3 to 4 hours. Strain and bottle.

APPLE SAUCE.

Pare and core six large apples, cut up, and stew half hour with small cup of water, then add small cup sugar, mash together with a wooden stirrer.

EASY BREAKFAST OR TEA DISH.

Stew gently some tomatoes with a little butter, pepper and salt, when soft mash with a fork, and add to them a well-beaten egg until they thicken. Serve on hot buttered toast.

SALAD DRESSING.

½ teaspoonful mustard
Pinch of salt
Little pepper
2 heaped dessertspoonfuls sugar
Yolks of 2 hard-boiled eggs

Mix all together, add sufficient milk (breakfastcup), then vinegar, stirring it until it thickens.

APPLE CHUTNEY.

4 lbs. green apples
2 lbs. onions
2 lbs. brown sugar
½ lb. raisins
2 teaspoonfuls salt
1 teaspoonful cayenne pepper
1 teaspoonful ground cloves
1 oz. garlic

Chop ingredients up fine (or put all through a mincer, except apples, salt, pepper, and cloves). Cut apples as for stewing, put all into pot, cover with vinegar, boil slowly 4 or 5 hours.

TOMATO SAUSAGE.

2 lbs. mutton, fat and lean (or any cold meat)
1 lb. tomatoes
¾ oz. black pepper
1 oz. salt, and little grated nutmeg

Put meat through fine mincer, mash the tomatoes, and rub through a sieve, removing skins. Mix meat and tomatoes together, add beaten egg to bind mixture, form into cakes, roll in flour, egg, and bread crumbs, and fry in boiling fat.

VEGETARIAN ROAST.

Bread
Peanuts
Milk, seasoning
1 onion

Brown some crusts of bread in the oven, shell peanuts and put them through the mincer, putting the bread through the mincer afterwards.

Take a cup of the bread crumbs, pour on them a little milk, just enough to moisten, but not to make them too soft.

Mix with them half a cup of the ground peanuts, salt, and a little powdered herb, either sage or thyme, and one minced onion, put all into a buttered pie dish, and bake slowly till nicely browned. If it appears to be getting too dry, a very little water may be put on top as it is cooking, or a few pieces of butter on top makes a fine improvement.

SAVOURY OMELET.

4 eggs
1 tablespoon flour
Large breakfastcup milk
Parsley, onion, salt and pepper to taste

Beat eggs, mix flour smooth with a little of the milk, then add remainder; stir into the eggs, add parsley, onion, pepper and salt; put a small piece of butter or dripping in frying-pan, pour in the mixture, and cook gradually. When brown underneath, cut in pieces, and turn.

HAM OR TONGUE OMELET,

Is made by adding about 2 tablespoonfuls of grated ham or tongue to the egg mixture, before it is cooked, omitting parsley.

COOKING HINTS

Cakes should be baked as soon as they are mixed.

Raisins should always be stoned.

Candied peel should always be thinly sliced.

For nice pastry, always sift the flour.

For scones and rolls, always use a very quick oven.

For buns and small cakes, a moderate quick oven.

For large cakes, not quite so quick.

For sponge cakes, a moderate oven.

Test the oven before baking—don't guess.

Before baking, have everything ready, and suitable fire.

Never slam the oven door when cooking, it spoils cakes, pastry, and puddings.

Two breakfastcups of flour piled up equal 1 lb.

Wooden spoons are better than metal for all cooking.

Always rub butter or lard into the flour with the fingers, not the palms of the hand.

Currants, sultanas, raisins, or sugar equal ½ lb. in barely level breakfastcup.

Edmonds' Baking Powder should always be mixed in dry ingredients, unless otherwise mentioned.

One breakfastcup of milk equals ½-pint; 1 teacupful of milk equals 1 gill.

A cake should rise before browning to its full height, especially sponge cakes.

You can always guess amount of butter to use in cooking by dividing the 1 lb. squares.

INDEX

Lector House believes that a society develops through a two-fold approach of continuous learning and adaptation, which is derived from the study of classic literary works spread across the historic timeline of literature records. Therefore, we aim at reviving, repairing and redeveloping all those inaccessible or damaged but historically as well as culturally important literature across subjects so that the future generations may have an opportunity to study and learn from past works to embark upon a journey of creating a better future.

This book is a result of an effort made by Lector House towards making a contribution to the preservation and repair of original ancient works which might hold historical significance to the approach of continuous learning across subjects.

HAPPY READING & LEARNING!

LECTOR HOUSE LLP
E-MAIL: lectorpublishing@gmail.com

9 789389 509779